Behind Her Brand:
Fierce and Fabulous at Fifty Plus

Compiled by Sherri Glisson

Co-authored by:

Sheila Grant

Denise Ackerman

Tamara Batsell

Leona Martin

Audrey Blake

Sherri Glisson

Behind Her Brand: Fierce and Fabulous at Fifty Plus
Copyright © 2015 by UImpact Publishing
All Rights Reserved

Behind Her Brand: Fierce and Fabulous at Fifty Plus
1. Self Help 2. Motivational & Inspirational

E-book Version: Kindle
ISBN-10: 069245618X
ISBN-13: 978-0692456187
Self Help/ Motivational & Inspirational

DEDICATION – THANK YOU

To woman everywhere that are fifty, or pretty close to it and older, continue to live your dreams and pursue your passions. To the many women in this age group who are still seeking to be the woman you envision when your eyes are closed, be encouraged to move forward, to live out your purpose and to realize that it is never too late. You possess the power to design your ideal life. You are strong, you are amazing, you are fierce and you are fabulous!

To the fierce and fabulous authors that helped to make this dream a reality by not only sacrificing your time but opening up the windows to your soul and exposing part of your truth, your story and your life, there aren't enough words to express what a blessing you all are.

To Kimberly Pitts and Melva Torres and Jatoya Akinyele of UImpact, thanks for all that you have done to bring this vision to life. You gals are simply FABUOLUS dahhlings!!

Fierce and Fabulous at Fifty Plus

TABLE OF CONTENTS

Sherri Glisson
Page 83

INTRODUCTION
BY: SHERRI GLISSON

I have the same essential needs as everyone else. We all possess the power to create the lives that we want to live, and we all have our scary monsters that come to attack us. The truth is, facing certain challenges at fifty and older is not the same as when you are a woman at a younger age.

I remember sharing with my young son, that he had a mommy that was much older than his classmates moms were. When I shared with him that I was fifty years old, he had the look of sheer shock on his face. He looked at me like I was an alien or something straight out of a dang horror show. We were sitting in his class where the little kiddos had prepared a cute Mother's Day snack for their moms.

He yelled out in sheer grief, "Oh my gawd, my mom is fifty!" Girl, all I could do was giggle at the embarrassment I felt when all of those cute little soccer moms whipped their heads around to look at me. Yes, look at me I thought to myself. I am a half a hundred years old, and I am FANTABULOUS okay? Ironically, this was the same time that I had begun my frantic hunt for the real Sherri. Will the real Sherri stand up, please?

Here we are five years after my rebirth at age fifty and I am proud to say, that I know who I am, and I have taken charge of my life. I finally understand what my individual role is in this drama and I want to get a standing ovation when the curtain closes.

My heart's desire is to help as many women as I can tap into their gifts and unleash their potential. I want to help them take center stage in their inspiration behind lives and that is the this book.

Fierce and Fabulous at Fifty Plus

Fierce Tip

Stand for what you believe.
Owning your no does not mean that you have to be loud.
Own it with humility, dignity, and grace.

SHEILA GRANT
Founder, Orijinz Salon

Tell us a little about yourself. We want to learn a little about your story.

As a child, I grew up in Dallas. I was fragile, timid and naïve. I was a loner, empty without cause and words. As long as I can remember, my mom was a victim of domestic violence in both marriages to my dad and step dad. She was shot four times in her beauty salon, by the hand of my step dad. Her life was taken at the age of 35 on February 4, 1981. I was in the fifth grade. It was the most traumatic experience ever, and it still hurts to this day. Long, long story short I ended up living on my own with two of my sisters. One of whom was two years younger and the other a year older. My eldest sister had just graduated from high school when my mom was killed, so she had already left for college. I was in the 10th grade. I have been living on my own ever since. I didn't graduate from high school up until now. I recently pursued and received my high school diploma this past January, 2015. It was important for me to share that part of my life because I realize it was my mom that set the foundation and the legacy of excellence and integrity in spite of the horrific pitfalls she encountered. I can remember her efforts of providing top notch services in a lavish upscale salon.

Life for me afterward was spiraling downward. My sisters and I experienced physical and mental abuse from my step mom. My dad was the one who decided that we should be out on our own because of the ongoing drama. He chose her over us. Of course, after I grew up I realized that my dad did all he could do with where he was mentally at that time and from where the course of his life had taken him. We experienced drugs, alcohol, dated Jamaican drug dealers that were big time criminals and we stole to survive. This is another book, and I can't expound on the details at this time but I learned life the hard way, and it got to the point to where I didn't want life anymore. I tried to commit suicide once and have had several thoughts afterward. One incident took place in my one bedroom apartment overlooking the pool, I was smoking weed, and my daughter was in the bed sleep. I climbed on to the gate covering my balcony contemplating the jump. I went up and down, changing my mind back and forth. Then I realized that I did not want to leave my baby girl all by herself for her to experience life without me as I did without my mom. Suicide has never crossed my mind since.

I married at the age of 19. The man I married was more like a father figure to me, which I had learned years after. I was drawn to the fact of having someone who was able to teach me the vital things of life that I didn't know existed. Like bills, and where to go pay them. It's like God used him to equip me with the things I needed for the next phase of my life which was to be a single parent.

We were married for seven years, separated for a few years and finally divorced when I was in my early 30's. That's when I truly started to see me as a person of existence in society. I started to discover my likes and dislikes. I was working for First City Bank, during the time I was married, for five years in item processing. I learned how the whole system worked from set up, proof, correction, sort, balance, and dispatch. I realized I was a quick learner and paid close attention to detail. At the same time I was working for the bank, I was also doing hair on the side. I would do hair during the day at home and work at the bank from four to midnight.

Share with us your dream and what you've done or are doing to make it a reality?

Well after the five years I was at the bank, Texas Commerce Bank bought us out. At that time I realized I wanted to start my own business. I knew they were going to be laying off, so I wrote my manager a letter, and I volunteered to be laid off. I let him know it would be a great opportunity for me to launch my own business. He granted it and provided me with my package that included my severance pay. The money helped me to attend beauty college full time as well as pay my bills. I completed beauty school in 1992.

I delved into the beauty industry full blast. As a single parent, I had to balance work and take care of my baby girl to provide her with the essentials of life. The business of doing hair chose me because I was good at it not to mention, my mom did hair, my step mom, and my sister. I attended some of the most elite classes of renowned celebrity stylists, on advanced cutting, coloring, and styling. Not to exclude weaving and extension techniques. I completed, attended and have been in many world class hair shows. Although I was successful at my business, the promotions , marketing,the whole nine. I didn't know how to DO business. It wasn't until everything slowed down, and I got used to all the attention because I knew I had it going on but I was empty inside, and I was missing something. It was a roller coaster, and I was running out of breath. You know how you're moving fast, but you're not getting anywhere. I was working from sun up to sun down with no purpose.

When did you discover your purpose?

I had a life changing experience. I became brand new at 32. Prior to 32, I had the mindset of thinking I could make it in life by myself. After my encounter with God and was saved by His grace, old things passed away and behold, all things became new, my heart changed. I started relying on God as my source, and I began to study His word. My desires began to change, and God delivered me from cigarettes, weed, and alcohol.

God began to teach me how to do business. He told me always to have water, candy and magazines for my clients. He taught me the principles of tithing and first fruits. The importance of honoring words that come out of your mouth. He showed me the importance of doing my best every single time, no matter what; even if I have only one client for that day. The scripture that always come to mind is Luke 16:10, whoever is faithful in very little is also faithful in much. I discovered that God is my purpose.

To allow Him to shine His light in the dark hidden places in my life, so I can be used by Him to tell others of His goodness and His saving grace.

How has living your purpose or making progress toward living your purpose affected your personal life?

God creates a harmony when you're truly where you are supposed to be. Romans 8:28 says it all works out together for good, to those that are called according to His purpose. Living out your purpose is a personal thing, so it's all connected. Being in business for myself has given me freedom to express and be who God has created me to be. Freedom to create an atmosphere that's conducive for my clients and my business. Freedom to allocate the time of operating hours around my family responsibilities and personal goals outside of my business.

If someone asked you, who would benefit from your calling, what would your answer be?

I believe it's a benefit for everybody, however, God gives us our gifts and talents. He has given me the ability to do hair and God uses that to carry out the mission he has given me to do. It's not just about the hair. It's also being a listening ear and showing love and compassion. I thank God for my clients, they understand me for who I am and appreciate what I have to offer. My clients are patient and know that I have their best interest at heart. They understand that I don't know all the answers but if they're out there, I will find them. I would think my clients that have been with me for a long time should know that they are my ideal clients' and that I love and appreciate them dearly.

How do you measure success and what is your definition of success?

I measure success with the scale of adversity because adversities will come, one after another. It's how you overcome those adversities. The attitude you choose to have often determines how long you remain in that situation. To me, success is choosing to press, not giving up and to show up at your post, anyhow. With the right attitude and the same quality of what you had to offer beforehand. Success is a progression of continuing to fight the good fight of faith, and it's in that you will see your dreams and goals begin to unfold.

What has been your biggest stumbling block along your journey to discovering your purpose?

The biggest obstacle I encountered since being in business is being true to myself. Standing and staying strong to what God has shown me as it relates to my business. For example, building boundaries around my business, if I worked a certain time frame and let my clients know I'm here for this time and that time, then I can't exceed that time. For the longest I allowed the clients to dictate when they wanted to get their hair done, and I was working the wee hours of the night. I didn't have time to refresh, think or regroup. I was all over the place struggling to care of my daughter and take care of my personal business. I overcame it because now I know the importance of having a strategy and a system in place to help make my business profitable, productive and my personal life peaceful.

Everything needs structure, even kids, I know my children are more happy and peaceful when there is order at home. Even our dog, Thor, my husband train him to potty outside, and when he decides to do it in the house everybody's mad. When there is a system in place, and you follow it, it works. There are times when you go against the rules, and you allow God to have His way. I innately know when God intervenes for His purpose. You make the adjustments, keep it moving and get back to the system. In addition to being true to myself, from experience, I realize God gave me my business, and I have a responsibility and I am committed to strive for excellence!

I remember making it a point to take care of everything I possessed. I considered it all a blessing. I would wipe everything down with germicides and bactericides. I would keep my working quarters clean and ready to go. I made sure I had everything I thought I may need to provide service because I don't like to run out of anything. I'm saying all of that to say, I wanted to maintain a certain standard, to create a clean atmosphere and a relaxing ambiance for my clients. I will always continue to think of ways to make my clients feel special and be more comfortable. If the clients are happy....business is good.

What have you learned about yourself during this journey?

It's funny the things you learn about yourself when operating your own business. I've learned that I like promptness. Matter of fact, I prefer to be at least an hour or so early because we all know time is never enough. I may get backed up sometimes when I'm working. However, I like to start on time.

The start of my day is very important. I like to prepare for the day. I fail sometimes, but I love to begin my day with thanksgiving, prayer, repentance and reflection. I pray for Gods' continual grace and mercy because I need and have to have Him. I pray that my choices please and glorify Him. I seek His guidance for each client. I want to know the best for that particular client. The hair care needs to be customized just for them. To help them look, feel and ultimately be their best. I look at my schedule for the day, observe each service and pull out what I may need for the day. I've learned that I'm about resolution. I don't spend a lot of time with the issue once I have determined the problem. I'm on a mission to research the problem, invest in what I may need to tackle the problem, whether it be time or money. Finally, to resolve the problem. One thing that stands out about me is that I'm all about time management. I meditate a lot on Gods' word on a daily basis. One scripture I think about periodically is Ecclesiastes 3:1, "to everything there is a season and a time to every purpose under the heaven". Most of the time, I practice managing everything I do according to time. Years ago God gave me a phrase that I speak to myself and that phrase is, *to capture the essence of now.* Ever since then, I strive to be mindful and thankful for everything under the sun, including time. My business is operating during the week. That's all the time I can allow. Again, there may be exceptions time to time, however when I'm away from the salon, I'm done with business. When I'm home, I'm enjoying my family and quality time with my husband and boys. I'm learning more and more each day to appreciate and use time wisely. One thing about it, once time is gone you can't get it back. I'm also conscious of maximizing time, and that means to kill two birds with one stone. I guess nowadays we call it multi-tasking. Sometimes I find myself cooking, cleaning while I'm on the phone listening to my voicemail, taking the dog out to potty, drinking coffee all at the same time. Most of the time when I have a task to do, I can only allow a certain amount of time. When that time is up, it's time to move on to the next thing. However, there are still times I will find myself in overload mode. I rely on the Holy Spirit to show me the things that need my attention the most, my priorities. I personally believe that you have to have balance with everything you do if you plan to be productive. I strive to stay true to my missions, and I encourage everybody to do the same.

What was your most rewarding experience since you began this journey?

It's such a rewarding experience when my clients get up from the styling chair with a new attitude. It's a testament to the mission being accomplished. A resurrection of expression is a new you. A woman to come in one way feeling kind of down and beat up from the storms of life and then to leave refreshed, empowered and ready to keeping fight. It's rewarding to see that I have a business that can transform a persons' life physically, mentally and spiritually. It's so rewarding to be able to listen and hear my clients' challenges and concerns. It's therapeutic for me because I'm able to listen to what I tell them and use it for myself. As well as them listening to my challenges and concerns and sharing their experiences and how they overcame. It's all part of Gods' purpose. It's also rewarding to read my customer reviews and see how they enjoyed their visit and services. Those are some of the things that help me press to be and do the best I can.

What three things do you now wish you would've known when things don't go right?

When I first started my business in my early twenties, I still had a lot of growing up to do, so my thinking wasn't beneficial for the development of my business. I guess at that time from where I was, it all happened the way it was supposed to. I wish I had known the benefits of having a financial blanket to cover me as a cushion for at least six months out. It would have better equipped me for taking my business to the next level, and it would have been less of a financial struggle. Also, I wish I knew when I first started my business the importance of separating my business finances from my personal finances. It was a headache during tax time because I had to go in and separate one from the other. Now looking back, I don't know how I didn't know to do that. I was learning as I go. Lastly, I started out wearing high heels every day, all day, for years. I did not own a pair of tennis shoes. So now that I'm older I wish I had started out wearing comfortable shoes, like SAS or Dr. Scholl's. If I had known that a little earlier in my career maybe I could have preserved my feet and maybe they won't be as sore as they are standing, and working all day.

How do you keep yourself motivated and encouraged when things don't go right?

When things don't go right, I keep myself motivated and encouraged when I reflect where God has brought me from. I know he didn't bring me this far to leave me. Gods' word promises us in Job 8:7 though the beginning was small, yet thy latter end should greatly increase. I think about the things that I have control of, and the things that are within my reach that I can change for the better. I've always believed if it's proven to be done; then I can do it and if it hadn't been done, it doesn't mean it can't be. It just mean that we can do all things through Christ that strengthens us. (Philippians 4:13). The things out of my control, I let go and let God handle it in His time. He's here to help us to know that we can't do it apart from Him. I'm also motivated through hearing and reading Gods' word. I know I have to catch myself sometimes when I'm allowing trials and adversities take over me, in my mind and my attitude because it will slip up in there and take you so fast you won't know what hit you. You will encounter that for a hot second but when you come to yourself, you realize that God got this. Nothing stays the same; you keep living, and things will change. It's just a matter of time. I believe it's so important to have the right attitude. An attitude of gratitude because it could always be worse. My biggest business goal over the next 12 months will be to expand my business. I recently made a financial commitment with WFAA Datasphere for one year to meet my goal. It's a marketing platform where a team of producers pulled together a vast of my business information and created a video, banner ad, and mobile website to reach out to millions of consumers. My goal is to get obviously more business through their networks. Like local saver, yellow pages, etc. I can see the potential growth for my business and I believe that will help take Orijinz salon to the next level. They've set up a user-friendly portal and created me a user ID and password. I use it to communicate with the producers, to upload and modify information. Also, to view the analytics to see how many consumers have looked at my business ad. It's laid out very professional.

What advice would you give to a woman in or near her fifties and older that wants to step out on her own and follow her dreams?

I would encourage a woman approaching her fifties or any woman that's ready to step out on faith and follow her dreams. My advice to you would be just to do it, time is now. We can talk about doing something and look up and it's three years later. God laid it on your heart to do. You already know what the to do is because you've meditated on it for the longest. If you have that inner peace about it, go for it because the word of God says in Colossians 3:15, to let the peace of Christ rule in your hearts. You'll tell yourself, well I'll do it when, whatever, whatever that is, and forget about it because life set in again. Then, there it is again. You have to step out at some point, do all your homework as it relates to your dream. Pull all your resources together, and don't let nothing hold you back. God didn't give us the spirit of fear, but of power, love and of a sound mind. (2 Timothy 1:7) You can do it!

One of the biggest struggles that women face when starting to pursue their dreams is dealing with the voices that tell them, "no." It's too late, "no one will support you"… etc. What is

the one thing that has helped you to overcome the battle of the voices and continue your journey?

Knowing the Word of God has helped me to decipher between the "voices". I have a voice, however, if it's not lined up with His word, I'll end up going back and forth, unsure of myself, hiding in a corner somewhere crying scared. If I listen to the devil, it will be deceit, one lie after the next. I would be getting dizzy because I would be going in circles. My head would be spinning, and I'll be looking crazy. In knowing His promises, I know there is always hope. Why…because He got up and hope came alive. So block those voices by meditating on God's promises and change your no to yes! One vital aspect while on your journey is knowing your self-worth. Only you can know the value of timeless hours you've spent researching, practicing and knowing your craft inside and out. Your experience through work and education is also a contributing factor in determining worth. Not to mention, thousands on top of thousands of dollars spent throughout your life towards your dream. When it's time to price your services and what it is you have to offer, all of those things I mentioned has to go into consideration. Also, consider the demographics of your business location, compare prices from businesses that may offer the same services that you may offer to see the ballpark prices that are out there. In addition, examine your expenses, the quality of products and services. In other words, you know your performance. Self-evaluate and write out pros and cons and be honest with yourself. In regards to knowing your strengths and weaknesses. It's also a good idea to ask close friends and family. Be open to corrective criticism from someone that you know is successful in their endeavors and have found a way to maintain a positive attitude. Someone that you know will be honest with you. I've had clients to tell me that they can go over to Shanaynay and pay less for a relaxer, but they fail to realize that she just started doing hair. What this means is she has less experience. She hasn't yet invested in continued education, so she can't possibly be measured up next to a veteran that has been in the field for over 20 years. So, consider your location, the services and products you're offering. Know your self-worth, do some comparisons and then you will clearly see how to price your services.

What must have resources/connections would you recommend?

There is one favorite, stand-alone book that's great for business, and everything else that pertains to life and that book is the inherent word of God. The bible, has tons of vital, applicable life principles that has been practiced, proven, tried and true. I love the book of Proverbs, it teaches wisdom, stature, perseverance, and integrity. Some of the main vitals needed as a foundation to succeed in life as well as, in business. I also recommend other resources such as *I am, I can and I will Walking By Faith*, by Joe L. Dudley, Sr. Also, *Start Your Own Business*, by Rieva Lesonsky. In addition to it all, I find keeping a journal can be used as a personal resource as well. To help serve as a track record for writing out short and long term goals. A tool for keeping up and reflecting timelines, things to do and the things you have done, all about your business. A handy place to keep personal notes and important information.

What does Fierce Fabulous at Fifty Plus mean to you?

To me being fierce, fabulous at fifty plus means to be a wise woman with a vision, pursuing excellence where nothing can distract her or stand in her way. A God-fearing woman that knows who she is and whose she is. A woman that knows what she want and need. Prepared to fight for what she believes in. A mother, a teacher, a wife, a sister, a server, a leader, a helper, a giver and a maker. A beautiful being, wonderfully made with perfection and wonder. A gift... a jewel. I'm not quite fifty but as I approach each day with thanksgiving at the grace and mercy of God, I can appreciate women that have gone before me and carried the torch to victory aspiring me not to give up. That has sacrificed themselves for something or somebody else. That I will too, leave a legacy to inspire others to be all God created them to be.

To be fierce, fabulous at fifty plus is a woman with knowledge, talents, gifting's and experience. She knows the ropes. The ones to stay away from and the ones to use to tie together to get to where she needs to go. In other words, she uses her stumbling blocks as stepping stones to rise to higher heights to get to the other side. She's a woman that builds her home and does not tear it down. She walks by faith and not by sight. She's loving, kind and compassionate. She is top of the line, yet humble in spirit. Don't mess with her, she is fiftyish, fabulous and fierce to the bone.

LET'S CONTINUE THE CONVERSATION
Sheila Grant

Sheila Grant is a professional coiffurist for over 25 years. She specializes in all textures of hair and provides an array of customized services for her clients. Orijinz Salon was established in 2003. The name Orijinz was inspired by God and is known for its exquisiteness of what it represents. It represents the servanthood and services provided to reaching **O**ut to empower women, **R**estoring while **I**mparting the love and hope of **J**esus with **I**ntegrity, **N**ourishment, and **Z**eal. Sheila currently resides in Frisco TX, with her husband, daughter, three boys and grandson.

Connect with Sheila:

Website:
www.orijinzsalon.com

Fierce and Fabulous at Fifty Plus
Fierce Tip

Don't feel intimidated by others who share their knowledge. Always try to look at things from a new a fresh perspective. You're never too old to learn. Don't be stingy with sharing your knowledge. Your wisdom will help make your world a better place.

DENISE ACKERMAN
Founder, The Radiance Coach

Tell us a little about yourself. We want to learn about the person behind the brand.

Every woman begins as a tiny essence growing within another woman's womb. Genetics may pre-determine how she will be in physical form but what lies unknown are her infinite possibilities. Thrust from the warm cocoon that is wrapped around her she struggles through the tight darkness into the intensity of the light that becomes her world, like a butterfly transforming to take flight. The tiny being screams at the rudeness and brightness that begins her life, her story.

Born to 19-year-old parents in Ft. Worth, TX, I was thrust into their world nine months after their wedding. The first of five born in six years, responsibility came to me almost as soon as I could walk. Overwhelmed and inexperienced, my mother did what she could to manage her quickly expanding brood. Depending on her eldest for help, I became the chief duckling leading the troops. Unprepared for the role of motherhood, my independent, artistic mom put her dreams and paint brushes away to change diapers and keep our tummies full. With determination and an innate love, she did the best she could do.

My grandmother and mother instilled deep faith in me. Sitting in a pew at seven years old, I knew then that I was being called. At that age, I had no idea what had moved through me but I knew there was something guiding my way. Fearing that I would walk the same path she had, marrying early and having babies, my mother vowed that would not happen. Using the money my dad had set aside for insurance, she sent me to college. Being a good Baptist girl, I'd felt God was calling me to be a missionary. I negotiated and instead became a social worker, impacting lives of broken families.

There have been many magical, almost unexplainable occurrence throughout my adult life. Leaping into real estate from social work was one of those. With little money to start my career, I'd almost naively jumped into it. Despite a severe dip in the economy, I had been able to not only sustain my life, my income as a single homeowner had also risen to being one of the top 20% agents in the real estate office where I worked. I loved being an entrepreneur. Even though I went through some lean times, the freedom and deep satisfaction with my work made it all worthwhile.

After eight years of being a single woman, I told the Universe that no matter what, I'd find a way to become a parent by the time I turned 38. I was almost 36, and I'd tired of the dating scene with its heartbreaks, or worse yet, long boring evenings with the wrong men. I grew tremendously in mind and spirit developing more self-love as I discovered a new spiritual path, studied books on manifesting and joined a women's support group focused on relationships with men. In the process, I created a list of traits I desired in my perfect partner, took off the ring I wore on my left ring finger and affirmed, "The next ring on this finger will be a wedding ring from my forever love".

With the house I'd just bought with a fellow real estate agent friend, my time was filled with renovating it and my career. I told my dear, wise friend Nancy, I was done with men for a while and was going to focus on becoming happy with me and my life. Her sage advice was to let go and just become friends with the men I met. She told me "What you need is a male buddy!"

As if my fairy godmother had been listening and waved her wand, the magic happened unexpectedly. Shortly after that conversation, Nancy called and invited me to a 4th of July celebration with her, her boyfriend, and her housemate, whom I pictured as older, fat, balding; in other words "middle aged". Why else would someone be a "housemate"? Thinking little of it, I decided to go. After all, I didn't want to spend the holiday by myself.

Fireworks began exploding the moment I met the "housemate". Not old or bald, he was lean, tanned, tall and handsome. My heart leapt at first site. I reminded myself he was just to be my "buddy". As the cool observer, I couldn't imagine he would be interested in me. I shrugged off my feelings and told myself he was a little too cocky for me. To my surprise, the evening was delightful. We spent the hours in constant bantering, conversation, and laughter. A year later Ronny* and I were married. *Not his real name.

Our first home was the house I had bought before we married. In an older neighborhood, my friend and I bought it to fix it up and sell it. Within two months of the purchase, both she and I had met the man of our dreams. When she moved out, the house became ours. A striking contemporary that was reminiscent of a Frank Lloyd Wright in the woods, I'd loved the serenity of the trees that surrounded it. One year after the purchase and around the time that Ronny moved in, our "house in the woods" had become the "marshy money pit" with leaking and flooding a regular occurrence when heavy rains would hit. With a declining real estate market, I knew we could not sell it, so we put countless dollars into patching it.

We lived there for 13 years, bringing our babies home and surrounding them with our love. Despite the plaque the house seemed to have, we were seemingly happy. The typical conflict of marriage and life would invade us on occasion, but our enduring, and deep faith in God and one another would always carry us through any storm. Like so many women of my generation, I'd been raised to follow the guidance of my husband. With a deep longing to be happily married and loved, I ignored the subtle signs along the way. Looking back now, I wonder if the house was telling me something.

After our daughter was born, and my husband began to travel, he encouraged me to give up selling real estate. Agreeing that it was probably best for our young family, I moved into real estate administration and then leadership. I missed having my own business and helping families, but I justified it by acknowledging that I enjoyed leading people too. The consistent paycheck created more financial stability, gave us benefits and I had the weekends free to be home with the family. This became even more important when we had our son, two and a half years later.

Our new little guy was a sensitive fellow. Separation for my daughter had been tough, but it seemed even worse for him. We both felt he might do better with more time around me. When our son was nearing three, I convinced Ronny to let me quit my job, proposing that it would allow me time to grow a craft business I had created giving us additional income. Perhaps later I could help him with his business. After adjusting our finances, we took the risk and for the next five, glorious years I stayed home.

When the kids were both in school, I put all my energy into being the consummate PTA mom. The epitome of an athlete, Ronny coached the kids in soccer, baseball, and basketball. I was always the team mom. When not involved in the kids' sports, I was found leading girl scouts and rounding up a Cub Scout leader for our son and friends. Our little community of parents and children was tight. It was a happy time for us all. There were times I would pinch myself that life could be so good.

It was during that time, one of the mom's asked me if I had ever considered becoming a coach. Puzzled, I couldn't imagine why she thought I would want to coach athletics. With a smile on her face she explained she wasn't talking sports. As an HR director of a large corporation, she told me about hiring professionals who came in to inspire, motivate and "coach" their employees, telling me about the coach she had recently hired. I reminded her of him. She'd seen me help people through life crisis as a friend, and believed I had an innate sense about people. With complete confidence in my ability, she hired me to coach some of her staff.

After my first paid coaching session and some investigation into this new field, I knew I'd found something that I was meant to do. The work pulled forth a passion, a gift I'd forgotten. While talking to the people I'd been hired to coach, I felt a wisdom unfold to me from a force that was almost unexplainable. The more I learned about this fascinating new field, the more I hungered to know. Devouring every book I could find, I began to search for this new thing called the internet. I found Thomas Leonard, a man who seemed to be at the forefront of coaching. Inspired and certain, I told Sammy I'd found my new career. The kids were growing older, and it was time I put my talents to better use.

As our daughter approached middle school, we decided it was time to move. Finding the perfect community and deciding to build a new home, we moved the following summer. Twice the size of our old home, we felt like children in a candy store as we wandered through the rooms of this beautiful house. Our excitement and the dreams we'd shared were finally coming true. From our front porch, we could watch our children play in the cul de sac, and share evening dinners looking out our expansive back windows at the glorious sunsets. Giddy with gratitude we basked in the love we felt for each other, our children and our home.

A month later, Ronny lost his job. We'd spent all our savings on our new home so we knew we'd have to make some adjustments. He suggested I'd have to go back to work and get a job. It was clear my coaching business would have to take a back seat. Relying on my past connections, I found a position in leadership in real estate. Sammy did what he could do to make ends meet until his career could get on track. The stress of our lives and the change for our children began to wear on us.

That month, the month before the fateful 9/11, I turned 50. Once again, like the time I gave up my career selling real estate, I would give up my dream. Putting my family first, my heart's desires and my life would have to wait.

The following ten years we remained in our home. Working as a manager for a large real estate company, I was able to contribute income and provide the benefits we needed for our family. The hours were long and over the years, my connection to my children was often interrupted by the demands of my job. To add fuel to the smoldering fire within, menopause began to heat up in me. The turbulent eruptions of anger triggered by the storm of changing hormones, only mirrored the eroding layers of emotions including resentment caused by giving up my dreams and suiting up each day to play out a life that was not who I wanted to be. I consoled myself by remembering what I was doing had a tremendous impact on the lives of the people I led and contributed to the life we were living with our family.

In time, Ronny began to build a new career and company for himself. Working from home, he enjoyed the freedom and later, the income being an entrepreneur can bring. It also brought a flexible schedule while I stayed working long hours at the office. Many nights I would come home exhausted as he headed out to the country club in his new luxury car to play tennis. He'd say "Don't worry about making dinner for me. Just make it for you and the kids. I'll get something at the club."

"Don't quit your job." The words seared through me like a laser beam stunning me. I couldn't imagine why my husband, who had always been my greatest supporter, was now pushing me back from my dream, the one I'd put on the shelf for us. He was making great money; the kids were older so now seemed to be the perfect time to make it happen. The call within me felt so deep that I knew it had to be more than dissatisfaction with life or work. So now why was he again telling me no?

There had been several odd happenings I'd noticed of late. Ronny had become withdrawn and humorless with me. Still affectionate in a more subdued way, he continued to tell me he loved me while speaking to me to me with a scowl on his handsome, tennis tanned face. Where was "Chili", my endearing, funny guy, the one who could swing me in his embrace and tickle my funny bone? It was almost eerie the change I had begun to see. His humor, his light-heartedness and the laughter between us had vanished.

Recently I'd noticed strange expenses showing up in our accounts. Hotel stays with in-room meals, evenings out at a restaurant I loved, but we never frequented. Asking what they were, his explanations always seemed logical and related to business. Something was off, and I couldn't put my finger on it. When I began seeing the same number over and over on his phone log, I knew in my gut something I didn't want to face. Asking him point blank if he was having an affair, he vehemently said "No." I chose to believe him.

Our lives had changed as the kids began to grow up. When our daughter left for college, our son began to spend time with friends or by himself. With him upstairs on his game console, most evenings were spent with Ronny in front of the TV watching sports in the family room while I spent time in the bedroom. The storms brewing were like an underlying grayness that pervaded our family like a poisonous fog.

Many nights after work I would sit alone on our big romantic bed we bought when we moved to our new home and pondered the nightmare of my life. How did I get here doing a job that I didn't love and feeling isolated and alone? What was wrong with me that made my husband, my love stay away? What caused this to happen? The confusion was only diminished by the heaviness in my heart.

After years of despair, I had to have a talk with myself. Who was this stressed out, overweight middle age woman I had become? I realized that somewhere in the doing of life and doing what Sammy wanted, I had lost me, my dreams and **my** life. Being his wife and mother to our children and a woman who worked too many hours, I recognized the "me" I had become was not the "me" I desired to be.

Ten years since we moved to our new home and a few days after my 59th birthday, Ronny tearfully told me he had decided to leave. He'd rented an apartment in Austin, a place we'd dreamed of living years before. Still sensing that something was terribly wrong, this final move broke my heart in two. A few days later, after our son returned from his first day of college, my husband announced to our children "we" decided to take a break from each other, and he was moving away. The heartbreak on their faces far out shadowed the one inside of me.

A year later, Austin became my home too. Driving over the hill on the freeway into the city, I breathed in the freedom of my new life. Leaving my old life and the past few years behind, it was time for me. With courage and faith, I took the leap to writing a new story and begin again.

What a year it had been since Ronny announced he was leaving. On top of his departure, the real estate market took a downswing and the office I had managed suddenly closed. After ten years with one company, I found myself without a job, a husband and then my home. Dealing with the loss too, the kids wanted to go their own ways. Suddenly, for the first time in 23 years, I was alone.

Being a Texas girl, I had always wanted to live in Austin. Maybe now was my time. It would be a fresh start! I dreamed of a small apartment overlooking the hills, a place to heal my heart.

And maybe I could return to coaching? With the little bit of money I'd get from the sale of our house, I could start over.

Earlier that summer, I went to look at apartments. Once again, a power greater than me began weaving a tapestry through my life. A chance connection made earlier that year in a coaching course was strikingly connected to another person I met a couple of months later. Both had a connection in Austin and set up an appointment for me to visit a top coach with a large real estate company. Having no expectations, I spent an hour with a delightful gentleman discussing how agents who are coached have a greater success record. Leaving the building, I reflected on how exciting it was to find a company where the vision was to empower. I'd never considered coaching in real estate before but why not?

A month later, my new life was beginning. The hills of Austin would be my daily view from my apartment balcony. A short drive through the hills would take me to my work as a full-time coach for Keller Williams Realty. Like a college graduate, expectantly on the brink of a new adventure, I was starting over with childlike excitement at the age of 60.

It's been over three years since destiny called me to Austin. The journey, although exciting in the beginning, was a sometimes a treacherous road winding along the long downhill curves through the valleys of grief. A mountain top high was the birth of my one and only granddaughter that brought me back to the Dallas area where I make my home in Frisco. With memories of my grandmother tucked sweetly in my heart, I knew I wanted to give the same kind of love to this tiny new child. She now calls me Mia.

Share with us your dream and what you've done or are doing to make it a reality?

My journey is not unlike many women's. Life transitions can bring many changes. My dream is to inspire others to see midlife as a starting place, a new beginning of the rest of your life. As "The Radiance Coach" I want to be the conduit to help you find your light and let it shine. I began moving in that direction when I became a certified DREAM® Coach in 2012 and since then my vision has been to touch and transform the lives of millions through coaching, speaking and writing.

When did you discover your purpose?

My calling came as a child. It was then I learned the song "This little light of mine, I'm going to let it shine…" From then to social work to real estate to now, I've always known I was here to serve. Creativity and spirituality have always been moving forces in my life. Blending all those facets about me came together when I discovered coaching.

How has living your purpose or making progress toward living your purpose affected your personal life?

For years, I gave my power, my life away. Not only has creating my dream brought me fulfillment, it continues to build and bring me a sense of direction that I know will last the rest of my life.

If someone asked you, who would benefit from your calling, what would your answer be?

Women (and men) over 40 who find their life has gotten off course. From children growing up, marriages changing, illness and/or job life or just the change in life we all go through, it's easy to look up and say "Where's MY life now?" My desire is to transform the negative concept of midlife and older from "the end of life" to the beginning of something wonderful.

How do you measure success and what is your definition of success?

Living on purpose is success for me. Seeing the transformation in lives created by the work I do, gives me the greatest sense of success and fulfillment.

What has been your biggest stumbling block along your journey to discovering your purpose?

Me. By giving my power away and allowing fear to rule, I lost my way. Like many, I sacrificed myself to make others happy. What I've learned in my journey is that when let ourselves go, we also give away the very essence of who we are.

I also want to add that starting over is sometimes not easy. Many women have known that experience. By having a clear vision of what you desire, you can hold to your dream and allow it to be the fire that creates the phoenix who rises out of the ashes of your life.

What have you learned about yourself during this journey?

Life is often our greatest teacher when sprinkled with a good dose of wisdom, acceptance, and forgiveness, I've learned even when life looks differently than imagined, happiness can still be the outcome. While planting new seeds to bring hope to my heart, my grief still caused me to live daily in gloom and loneliness, spreading it around me like the smell of manure in the field of my dreams. A dear friend gave me great advice one day and said "The more you tell that story, the more you live it. Create a different story."

Often our stories define us. Telling the story can be cathartic, or it can be a trap; your healer or your greatest vice. How you tell your story will determine how your life will unfold. The lessons you learn from seeing and accepting what was can often determine the course you will take in the next chapter. Like digging for diamonds within the coal, it can be a catalyst to find the sparkle within. The magic happens when we acknowledge the guidance within, forgive and choose again.

If you see yourself in any place in my story, in the suffering and the blame, ask yourself "How long are you willing to tell your old story?" No matter the source of pain, we all have stories of life not happening the way we planned. Holding on to the past pain keeps us locked in the nightmares when the daydreams of brighter days escape us because we do not allow the light to come in. What happens when you change your story can change everything. You are the creator of your destiny.

What was your most rewarding experience since you began this journey?

Knowing I have been a catalyst for the transformation of lives is my greatest reward. From single moms to single young women, to midlife men and women their stories and new life stories continue to amaze me and are jewels in my heart.

What three things do you now wish you would've known when you started?

1. Stay true to yourself. No prince in shining armor or anything outside you will be the answer to "saving" your life. Don't let someone else be the ruler of your life and take away your power and vision.
2. Trust yourself. Listen to the inner guidance you are given. Watch the signs in your life, both positive and negative. If something feels off, it usually is. Trust your heart and your greatest desires for it is in them, the magic of you can be found.
3. Love yourself. Forgive and let the past stay there. Be grateful for today. Look into the future. Embrace who you are and go for it!
• How do you keep yourself motivated and encouraged when things don't go right?

I learned years ago that "What you focus on expands" from the great teacher Dr. Wayne Dyer. Meditation, visualization and focusing on my dream helps me stay focused. Vision boards can be found in my home and office. A lifelong learner, I attend at least one inspiring seminar or class a year.

What advice would you give to a woman in or near her fifties and older that wants to step out on her own and follow her dreams?

Just do it! If your fear or uncertainty gets the best of you, hire a coach.

One of the biggest struggles that woman face when starting to pursue their dreams is dealing with the voices that tell them "no", "It's too late," "no one will support you." Etc. What is the one thing that has helped you to overcome the battle of the voices and continue your journey?

Get clear about your purpose and vision for your life and stay focused with a "burning desire". There can be many naysayers in our lives disguised as friends and family. Choose carefully who you share your dreams with. Surround yourself with those who will truly love and support and believe in you and your dream.

What must have resources/ connections would you recommend?

Other women, good friends who support your new direction are the key to moving forward. Find others who want to continue to grow. I've had several coaches over the years who were my champions, so find a great coach who can inspire and truly hear and believe in you.

What does Fierce Fabulous at Fifty Plus mean to you?

It's a new beginning of the rest of your life. With great self-care and soul care, you can get "younger every year"! The best is yet to come!

LET'S CONTINUE THE CONVERSATION
Denise Ackerman

As a certified DREAM® Coach and as The Radiance Coach, Denise is an inspiring, heartfelt coach, speaker, and writer. Her vision is to touch the hearts of millions to live passionately and authentically. She has facilitated women's workshops and retreats on "The Artist Way" by Julia Cameron and other creative, inspiring works. Believing that we all have radiance within, she works with individuals and groups to let their "light" shine no matter their age.

Connect with Denise:

- Website – www.theradiancecoach.com
- Twitter- www.twitter.com/coachdeni
- Facebook - www.facebook.com/denise.s.ackerman

Fierce and Fabulous at Fifty Plus
Healthy Tip

Take care of your body....get up and move! Walk, dance while mopping or sweeping the floor, break out the hula hoop...girl just get your body in motion!

Your emotional and mental health is also your responsibility. Determine your stressors and find ways to eliminate them. Seek help if you need to. If you have to distance people that are causing you grief, remember you can still love them from afar. Don't take on more than you can handle without becoming stressed.

Fierce and Fabulous at Fifty Plus
Intentional Tip

Set goals that are realistic and time bound and put them in a place where you can see them. Align yourself with an accountability partner or group to help you stay on task.

TAMARA BATSELL
Founder, TB Style Works

Tell us a little about yourself. We want to learn about the person behind the brand.

I'm a 50-plus aged divorced, single woman with no children living in Dallas, TX. I was raised in the Midwest by a two parent home. I am the youngest and have two sisters. Education was big in our household, both my parents had degrees, and they stressed learning. They instilled in me a strong work ethic, high standards and "to do things right the first time". I played sports all my life and later into college which helped me to be strong both in mind and body. As a kid, I was often "bullied" due to my awkward appearance: tall, acne, braces, skin color, and more. I spent a lot of time reading fashion magazines and watching TV shows dealing with beauty trying to find ways to make myself pretty. As time went on I created my own sense of style through what I'd learned and by watching my mother who had a fabulous fashion IQ. When I was in college, I decided to put my height to use and went to Modeling School followed by some modeling work. Towards the end of college, I started working with the special needs population that blossomed into a passion for serving others. What followed was a 30+year career in Human Services. I moved to Dallas in my late 30's because I felt like I was missing out on life by living in the slow pace city of Topeka, KS. I have always been an entertainment seeker and loved going to concerts/plays, sporting events, fashion shows, and traveling. Dallas offered all of this, and

I soon became involved in the fashion culture while working full time in social services. I also went to makeup artistry school, did promotional modeling and provided styling for fashion shows.

Share with us your dream and what you've done or are doing to make it a reality?

My dream is to make a difference during my time here on earth. Having worked in the human services for such a long time and providing assistance to hundreds of families and clients, I felt it was time for me to shift energies in another manner. I shifted into the world of fashion.

My dream is to become a Fashion Connector. A person who can help you find your personal style, locate fashion sources, provide expert advice, and inspire people to live their best life with style. I dream of visiting different countries and speaking to women of all ages and races about self-worth and the importance of valuing how you present to the world. I decided that blogging would be a good fit for my dream. I could offer my voice of experience and be able to provide a large array of fashion resource. My first order of business was to start networking within the fashion/blogging community. I began searching online first and discovered a free webinar on how to become a successful blogger. After that webinar, I was even more convinced this was my calling. Next I found a Dallas blogging group on Facebook and started participating in discussions and attending local events. It didn't take long before I was asked to style for local fashion affairs. I was loving meeting all the new people and various opportunities, but I knew I had to get a blog going soon, but I needed to find my "niche" to separate myself from all the thousands of other blogs the world. I one day searching for "fashion for the over 40 woman" and I was shocked by how little information was out there. Bam! That's where I could share my voice and expertise. I decided at the age of 52 to start a fashion/style blog targeting the mature woman. Becoming a blogger is an eye opening experience but fellow bloggers have been very helpful. Although this is my passion I can't forget it's a business. I'm learning you have to educate yourself on how to make money through your passion. How do you monetize your ideas? We all have to eat and pay bills so be mindful that great ideas are valuable, get paid your worth. Reading and gaining knowledge from a variety of sources is imperative. I'm constantly online researching about blogging; who are the top blogger, what content is important, and how to establishing a relevant blog. Do your homework!!!

When did you discover your purpose?

Early in life I discovered that I wanted to help others. It gave me such a great feeling to know that something I did helped someone. Having worked with special needs and persons with disabilities for some years, I saw first-hand how powerful finding needed resources can be. I will never forget the time I was able to find a vendor that custom made wheelchairs for children. The client was a small child that had multiple medical conditions and a severe curvature of the spine that made sitting in their wheelchair very uncomfortable. The parents were very frustrated with seeing the child in pain whenever the wheelchair had to be used. After measurements and several fittings, the customized wheelchair was finished. That day is stuck in my memory banks, and I will never forget the huge smile that broke out on the child's face when placed on the shiny metallic blue chair, custom fit to specifications. The parents were so happy, and the mother hugged me in appreciation. That's the moment when I knew being a resource to others was "my calling".

I first felt my styling purpose when women would stop and ask me about what I was wearing or when ladies shopping would ask me for styling tips. That is when I started seeking out events that needed a stylist. I discovered I had a good "eye" for what looked good on various body types.

I feel powerful in my purpose when I help a woman find her groove....swag...diva, or whatever you want to call it. When she walks out that dressing room and she sees herself in the mirror and says," I look pretty" My heart kinda melts when I hear this. Many women today don't feel good about themselves due to the unrealistic images that the media portrays. The ability to assist someone in feeling good about themselves not only on the outside but on the inside is very gratifying.

How has living your purpose or making progress toward living your purpose affected your personal life?

Most of my life, I have been a very positive upbeat person, but discovering my purpose and creating a new path has brought me joy. My life has expanded; I am meeting new people, and then they are introducing me to new people...it's kind of like a ripple effect. I'm feeling more capable as a person as my purpose becomes clearer.

My life feels more energized. I wake up with so many ideas and projects on my mind. You find the energy that you didn't think you had because you know things have to get done. Life with a purpose has more color, things just don't look the same when you are purpose-driven. I find that life has to be a little more scheduled due to more meetings and other duties. I'm not as carefree as I use to be, and now I really do have to look at my calendar before committing to anything.

I've learned to say "yes" to things that scare the crap out of me, but somehow it all turns out alright. I can't explain, it but once you have focus and clarity the fear lessens. I'm not saying that it goes away but taking that first step is easier.

Making progress towards my purpose has introduced me to some amazing women doing awesome work. I find myself in admiration of the great accomplishments local business women. I follow these women on social media and various other platforms to gain as much knowledge as I can. Everyone has a story, and I know "all that glitters ain't gold". Having a mission and goals come with a sacrifice and not everyone will understand but you have to keep your eye on the prize. I've had to gain discipline in my life to meet deadlines. I have also found out how important it is not to procrastinate because time is money.

If someone asked you, who would benefit from your calling, what would your answer be?

- The woman that is wanting to take her life to the next level and is tired of the same ole look but doesn't know where to go or what to buy.

- Women's organizations that are business oriented and embrace the importance of personal enhancement.
- Mothers groups that want some resources on styling after giving birth, or who are looking to revamp an outdated wardrobe.
- The mature woman who wants ageless/timeless style that reflects who she is but doesn't know where to go or what to wear.
- The woman who is budget conscious but wants to get the most style for her money. I shop sales and believe style doesn't have to be expense.
- Media outlets seeking a fashion connector with the pulse on fashion trends, styling various body types, and good social media content.
- Brands are seeking a fashion/style ambassador to represent the modern mature woman.
- Professional women's group that seek advice on style presence and the appropriate wardrobe for corporate America.
- Businesses are seeking training about professional attire in the workplace.

How do you measure success and what is your definition of success?

I define success but being able to follow your heart's desires and live a life of joy, prosperity, and love. My personal success would include personal happiness and making a difference in as many lives as I could. I know that money can't buy happiness, but I would consider personally financial comfort and stability a success.

Success to me is about being at the top of my game along with finding value and worth in what I do and offer to others. I'm not sure about measuring success because that seems to minimize the amount.

Success is about freedoms; free to travel when you want, free to make your own schedule, free to say no, free to spend more than you expected, and free to speak your mind even though it may cost you.

What has been your biggest stumbling block along your journey to discovering your purpose?

My biggest stumbling block along this journey has been, ME. I have doubted myself, seconded guess if I was doing the right thing and just overall delayed the progress. The mind can play tricks on you if you allow it. At times, I find myself so stuck I just escape by not thinking about all that needs to be done and escape into mindless television or other unproductive behavior.

What I've learned that works for me is writing things done and using a calendar, especially one that has an alert. It may not work for everybody but if I see it in writing on a specific day and hear the alarm I feel pressured to get it done. Fear is also a HUGE stumbling block. Fear of failure, fear of what others will think, fear I'm not good enough, and even fear of success. All of these are excuses, and I have started treating them as such. I grew up with parents that did not accept excuses; you took responsibility, and then you corrected the problem. That is the mentality I am developing to eliminate the fear and to push forward.

Finances can be an obstacle but if you're willing to sacrifice time, pleasure, and the "wants" you can meet your goals. There will be times when you are not able to "go out and play". I've had to say no to some outings. Doing things that give you pleasure may need to be put on hold for a while. Limiting manicures and pedicures, shopping, and eating out are all things that can help to boost the bank account and fund a passion.

What have you learned about yourself during this journey?

I've learned that I'm more powerful than I thought. I've learned I need organization to function well. Structure is very important for me to be successful on various projects. Although I love being creative it's necessary for me to streamline dates, times, deadlines, and duties.

I've learned I can't do this alone. You have to reach out to people for help whether it be a friend or a paid consultant. Also, I've learned to speak up and seek out resources because you never know who knows who.

Pursuing a passion can be lonely at times. I've felt alone and wanting companionship to share this journey with. As a single woman with no children, you learn to embrace your time alone but lonely is a different feeling. What I've learned to do during those moments is to look at my surroundings and count my blessings. I have shelter, I have people who love me, I'm in good health, I have money in the bank, and God has graced me with life. So the "pity party" doesn't last long, and I've learned I'm pretty tough mentally.

I've learned I was a brand and didn't even know it. I once heard branding described as "The process by which we market

53 | Page

ourselves to others". I am loyal, creative, genuine, accountable, insightful and have a story to tell...sounds like a good brand to me.

What three things do you now wish you would've known when you started?

1. I wish I had known that it didn't take a lot of money to start your own business or pursue your passion. Just start with what you love to do and are good at. Then start writing down ideas, don't limit yourself. Begin to educate yourself by attending various event, seminars, and/or sign up for free online courses. I had no idea there were so many experts in various fields that provide free webinars for beginners in various industries.

2. I wished I had known I had the right stuff! What I mean is that I'm capable of achieving more than I thought. I wish I had more confidence in myself to "go for it" earlier in life. But I truly have no regrets, because I'm exactly where I need to be at this time. You have got to believe in yourself and don't expect to get validation from others. Be your own cheerleader and do things for the right reason, not for accolades or fame.

3. I wish I had known how much fun and exciting this journey would be. It's a joy to follow your passion and get results. Is it hard work? Yes. Learning new things, meeting new people who embrace you and support your passion is uplifting. Creating a project from beginning to end and seeing it manifest is very satisfying. I have met some people in the fashion industry whose path I wouldn't have crossed in a million years if I hadn't decided to start my journey.

How do you keep yourself motivated and encouraged when things don't go right?

Staying motivated can be a visual thing for me. I sometimes cut out pictures or save images on my phone to look at when I'm feeling uninspired. I love to travel so I have a picture of The Maldives (a tropical paradise) saved on my phone as a reminder of a travel goal. I have notebooks full of quotes I have gathered over the years. When I'm feeling a little down or defeated, I pull them out for encouragement. One quote reads; "Life begins at the end of your comfort zone"- author unknown.

It may be strange but working out keeps me motivated. On the treadmill/stairmaster is when I do some of my best thinking and exercise positive affirmations. I tell myself I can do better, and I will do better. I strategize on what is necessary to complete my next goals.

Also what helps me stay encouraged is to be mindful of success stories that almost didn't happen. The story of Colonel Sanders of the famous KFC is inspiring, he endured over a 1,000 rejections before finally finding a restaurant that would work with him. Then there's the story of one of the greatest basketball player ever Michael Jordan and how he didn't make his varsity basketball team until his junior year in high school. These examples of perseverance give me hope that if I work hard enough, create a strong brand and fine tune my skills there is no limit to my success.

What advice would you give to a woman in or near her fifties and older that wants to step out on her own and follow her dreams?

Ask yourself, do you want to leave this earth with regret that you didn't follow your heart? I hope you answered, no. Women in their late 40's and 50's are often people who know who they are and are not easily swayed by common opinion or peer pressure. This perspective needs to be heard. Your time to "shine" and share your gifts is now. Baby boomers numbers are large and in charge. The numbers of 40-plus aged women are huge and businesses are starting to recognize their buying power and looking for brands that can relate to this age demographic.

It's important to be active in the community and become involved in activities, groups, Meetups, or anything connected to your passion or purpose. I find it helpful to be around people younger than myself. They can offer a fresh perspective on issues and assist with keeping your creative juices flowing. Try to learn new ways of doing things. Sometimes the old way is not always the best way. Embrace modern technology as much as you can, some duties/tasks can be greatly reduced but learning new apps or programs.

Your time is now to pursue the dream. Put down the fear and pick up your passion.

One of the biggest struggles that woman face when starting to pursue their dreams is dealing with the voices that tell them "no", "It's too late," "no one will support you." Etc. What is the one thing that has helped you to overcome the battle of the voices and continue your journey?

The one thing that has helped me to overcome the battle of negative voices is my self-worth. I have frequent talks with myself about what I'm deserving of. I believe I deserve respect, love, kindness, consideration, attention, and to be happy in my own skin. Self-worth is something that I have gathered over time and has served me well. I feel good about who I have become and where I'm headed. Have I made mistakes and done stupid things to myself and others? Yes, I have, but I can't continue to beat myself up for what is done. We have to overcome our mistakes and disappointments and turn them into life lessons that strengthen us.

I feel good at the age of 52 and want to let others know that I'm kicking the rocking chair off the porch! The voices of "no you can't do that at this age" I ignore. All of my life experiences haven't been in vain, I'm stronger due to what I have been through, and age has diminished my need for acceptance.

Be prepared that no one in your immediate circle may support your purpose/passion. This happens, and you have to remain strong in your pursuit. There are many online groups and local community organizations that will offer you support and guidance. You are not alone, and it's important to seek out others that share your interest.

What must have resources/ connections would you recommend?

At the beginning of my journey, I started looking for a resource on how to blog. I came across free webinars exactly on this topic. On Facebook, I constantly see a variety of free webinars on a variety of topics. I strongly recommend signing up for one.

- Join an online community/group similar that can help you with your purpose. You don't have to get dressed or drive in order to get the information.

- Become more social either online, in-person or both, socialization is important. It may be uncomfortable at first, but people love to talk about themselves. You never know what people do for a living or how you may be a resource for one another.
- Be a presence on whatever social media platform works best for your passion.
  - Instagram
  - Pinterest
  - Facebook
  - Twitter
- The Better Business Bureau in your community offer classes on various topics that can be helpful. Check them out online and look on their calendar for events/classes.
- Find a business coach that can help tailor your dream/passion into a well-designed plan. Ask other business people you trust for recommendations. Or just research online and find one that matches your wants and desires.
- Mailchimp.com- email marketing service
- Paypal.com-online payment system
- Reddit.com-entertainment, news, & social networking site where members can submit content
- Dropbox.com-a free home for storage of all your photos, docs, videos, and files.
- Liveminutes.com-a free real-time platform for project management, document sharing, and traditional web-conferencing
- Picmonkey.com-free photo editing, fix photos and create outstanding graphics.

What does Fierce Fabulous at Fifty Plus mean to you?

Fierce-showing a heartfelt and powerful intensity. I think that pretty much sums up what I feel about being in my 50's. My love for life is more heartfelt, and I feel more powerful within my spirit than ever before. Time seems to have flown by. I often find it hard to believe I am 52 years old. I can honestly say that I do feel fabulous in my 50's. I have few aches or pains and besides my reading glasses not much has changed for me since my 40's. I do realize I am truly blessed with great health. I try my best to maintain a healthy lifestyle by working out, eating right and maintaining a positive attitude.

Fierce Fabulous and Fifty Plus means to me that what I find to be my normal is not normal at all. I've felt fabulous most of my life and hope to continue to feel fierce for many years to come. I don't subscribe to limiting my life, activities, or style due to my age. Life is to be lived, and that is what I'm doing. I travel as much as I can, I laugh probably more than the average person, I still believe in being silly, and most importantly I enjoy being me.

I feel too many fifty plus women have given up on life. I hope I'm not over generalizing, but it's important to stay vibrant and adventurous. Try new things, go new place, wear color, and don't be put in a box by what society expects of you at 50 plus. If you can still wear a 4'inch heel and a pencil skirt put it on! If your desire is to skydive at 60, get on that plane and enjoy the air. Enjoy the life you have been given at 50 plus, it is a blessing... the fabulous and fierce is just icing on the cake.

LET'S CONTINUE THE CONVERSATION
Tamara Batsell

Tamara refuses to let age define her. She is a 50 + woman who is feeling fine and just hitting her stride. Her work history is diverse, from fashion to human services. A self-proclaimed "fashion gal" she doesn't take beauty industry standards too seriously. She believes "Beauty fades but style is eternal".

Tamara recently started a fashion/lifestyle Blog (TBstyleworks) full of inspiration, style tips, fashion and most importantly loving yourself at any age.

Connect with Tamara:

- Twitter: tbstyleworks
- Facebook: tamara.batsell.1
- Instagram: tbstyleworks
- Google: Tamara Batsell
- Pinterest: tbstyleworks

Fierce and Fabulous at Fifty Plus
Grounded Tip

Take the time to just be still. Find time to be quiet where you can meditate and be alone with your spirit.

Find yourself an accountability partner, mentor or coach. Someone that will help you stay on task, stay on target, and stay true to yourself. So many women are all over the place doing everything for everybody and end up losing themselves. Having someone to hold you accountable will prevent this from happening and help you to live a more fruitful and productive life.

Fierce and Fabulous at Fifty Plus
Courageous Tip

Feel the fear and do it anyway. Remember without fear there wouldn't be a need for courage.

Focus on where you want to be….the goal. Let the end result, the thing that you want to achieve be the driving force, the magnet that pulls you forward in spite of the fear.

LEONA MARTIN
Founder, LCM Career Coaching

Tell us a little about yourself. We want to learn about the person behind the brand.

I am married and have two beautiful daughters and two awesome grandchildren. I have a loving husband who supports me in everything that I do and has been my rock over the past 18 years. I wish I had met him 40 years ago. He is calm, understanding and has a heart of gold. I have a wonderful extended family with two brothers and two sisters all living in Massachusetts as well as many nieces and nephews who I love and adore. My family has kept me grounded and motivated to keep growing and developing in my career and my overall life. I was never one who would be satisfied with the status quo, I always was striving to do more and would get bored pretty easily. Whenever I felt that I had reached that plateau in a job, it was time to move on to do more things that challenged me, kept me interested and broadened my knowledge. I possess a spirit of strength, love and compassion for everything I do.

I have worked in the field of human resources for over 20 years now and have worked in various industries. I got into the field because I am truly a people person. I have held various roles in the field of human resources, but I have loved the work I've done as a recruiter. I worked in the high-tech industry and then moved to the healthcare industry where I discovered that recruiting and mentoring were real passions for me. This is what I looked forward to coming to work every day to do "match the right people to the right jobs". I worked as a nurse recruiter for about 12 years and loved this population of people. I also feel blessed and very fortunate that I was able to learn about the healthcare industry in depth especially since I had wanted to be a nurse since I was in elementary school. I found it amazing that I ended up working with the group of people that I wanted to be a part of. I did not end of up being a nurse because I had my first daughter while still in high school and had to put college on hold. However because I had a very strong and supportive mom, I was able to finish high school, work part time and think more about what I wanted to do given the demands of being a young single parent. I had the most loving Mom and Dad, and I don't know where I might be if it hadn't been for all the love and support that they gave me. I also had a great extended family as well, and when I was growing up, it really did "take a village". I was the oldest of 5 children, and we lived in a small apartment with not much money but lots of love.

I decided that I wanted to work at one of the most prestigious colleges in Massachusetts. It was there I learned from some of the smartest people in the world which developed my work ethic, customer service skills, and just a passion for being the best at whatever it is you do! I attended college at night and worked during the day for many years, always learning new things, meeting great people and supporting my family. My oldest daughter was exposed to so many great things and great people and all the while, discovering that God had a plan for me and my family. Although there were some difficult times, we persevered and never looked back or gave up. The fact that I was a young single mother never kept me back, and I never used it as an excuse not to get and do what I wanted in work and in life. I was able to be a positive role model for her, and now she has grown into a beautiful, loving mother to my two grandchildren.

I enrolled in a master's program when my first daughter was a teen and obtained my degree in education while working full time during the day. I attended the four classes a semester at night for 18 months in an accelerated program for working adults. It was a challenge to attend school; work during the day and provide for my daughter, but I was determined to get this done. Again, there I was reaching for the sky. I thought at this point in my life I wanted to be a trainer and teach classes at the corporate level. I was working in the high tech industry at this point in my career. The unfortunate thing about this was that once I completed by program and obtained my degree, the company started downsizing so the opportunity to be a trainer was not a reality. It was disappointing. However, it was another goal that I completed, and I knew it would benefit me if not then sometime in the future.

All the work and things that took place those years were building character and confidence I never knew I had. I built the strength and courage to keep pursuing all that life had to offer. I worked for several employers over the years. However one day I started thinking about how my long work commute, long work days and stress were starting to wear me down. I thought to myself it's time for a new direction and that something had to change. Both my family and I were experiencing the pain of me being away from home too long and too often. I had another daughter who is now a teenager who needed me to be home more than I was there. She has some learning challenges, and it was critical that I and not just my husband be there for her every day to support and nurture her. She is my pride and joy—she has so many talents that she has yet to unleash. People think that because of her challenges, she is not able to do things but my husband and I know better. All she needs is support and encouragement since she is not your traditional learner. She learns differently but has the desire and the motivation to succeed. I will leave no stone under turned in getting her what she needs to be successful. The teenage years are very crucial for the growth and development of any student whether with or without learning disabilities. I will not allow any school or organization to dictate her life.

Share with us your dream and what you've done or are doing to make it a reality?

So, my dream has been to start my career coaching practice. I realized that since I had all this recruiting and coaching experience, wouldn't it be great to work for myself, make my own hours AND have time to spend quality time with my family! Also, I came to the realization that I no longer wanted to have corporate America dictate to me how I would earn a living. I also realized that there were so many young people that need help and support in looking for jobs, writing resumes, and how to market themselves. I felt that I had to do something to motivate, encourage and help build confidence in those people who were having difficulties or challenges of seeking jobs that they looked forward to going to every day. I have been having much success with my clients as a career coach. I feel that I've been making a difference in the lives of many professionals both new grads and experienced in achieving their career goals! My success rate is high, and I am proud of what I've been able to do for my clients.

When did you discover your purpose?

I know my purpose is to enable those who aspire to do great things with their careers. I discovered my purpose by the success I've had over the years with helping and serving people from all walks of life. I was drawn to encouraging people never to accept "don't" or "can't" and that if you work hard you can do anything you set your mind to. As a result, I've received many referrals from those people I have worked with who have been successful in reaching their goals while working with me.

How has living your purpose or making progress toward living your purpose affected your personal life?

Living my purpose has broadened my whole outlook on how I live my life. I don't allow the word "can't" in my household, and positive thinking and discussions are the only things I encourage in my home. I am always in a "living your dream" mode with family and friends. I'm always encouraging my kids, grandson and nieces and nephews to pursue their dreams and to never let anyone ever break their spirits. I encourage them to dream big and to keep striving for the best. I tell them to be your best self in everything that you do and don't be discouraged! Anytime that I speak to someone who is looking for growth and development in their workplace and/or is looking for a new job, I give them pointers on how to get started. I am always reading up on new trends. Just anything new on how to market one's skills, what the hot industries are, and anything else that I know would help someone looking to advance in his or her career. Personally, all this has inspired me to keep doing what I love, share it with my family and friends and to live a full life. I always encourage my children and grandchildren to seek the very best life has to offer. It has also encouraged me to not sit on my spiritual gifts and to be a role model for those in my community who may need my help.

If someone asked you, who would benefit from your calling, what would your answer be?

If someone asked me who would benefit from my calling, I would have to say anyone who aspires to do great things in their career and wants a job that they love and look forward to going to every day. I am someone who loves to motivate, encourage and help people reach those career goals by staying focused on what it is they are trying to achieve. Others that would benefit from what I do are those who really need a push and need an accountability partner to help them stay on task with their goals and to develop a plan of action that they can stick to. I also have a track record in helping people find jobs in a short period of time. I save people time and stress by cutting down on the time it takes them to find that right job vs. what time it would take if they were looking on their own.

How do you measure success and what is your definition of success?

My definition of success is when I am doing something that I enjoy, and I am happy and stress-free and know that I am making a difference in the lives of others. I measure success by feeling good about where I am in my life and that I am accomplishing the goals I've set for myself. I can "check things off" on my goals list. While money is important to me, I feel like success is more than having lots of it. We all know that some of the richest people are not happy, and happiness is a part of success for me.

What has been your biggest stumbling block along your journey to discovering your purpose?

I think the only stumbling block I've had is myself! It's been hard to get out of my "own" way along this journey. I learned that I have knowledge that people will pay for. They will as long as I help them to understand what is needed to be successful in the job search and ways in which to find your dream job. I have also learned that I can do so much more than what employers gave me credit for. I also learned that the fear I had inside of me when I started this journey was erased when I allowed my faith to kick in and to trust and believe in myself. What I find when working with clients is that if people would look inside themselves and see all the talent they have inside, it's easier to bring out the best in yourself. Having self-confidence is the key to anyone's success.

What have you learned about yourself during this journey?

I learned that I have much to offer and that I have to step out on faith every day. I also learned that I must allow myself to be uncomfortable sometimes to grow and develop further in my business. I've learned how difficult it can be to get into uncomfortable territory, but the rewards can be endless.

What was your most rewarding experience since you began this journey?

The most rewarding thing since I started this journey has been all the people who I have helped find good jobs! Next would be that I have flexibility with my time and that I'm finally in charge of my own destiny. It is truly a beautiful thing to be able to make your own schedule from week to week. However, you have to be disciplined to stay on task and stay focused. Being in your home office is far more challenging than being in an office at a job site. So, having that flexibility is great but you must stay on task.

What three things do you now wish you would have known when you started?

The three things I wish I had known when I started this journey are the following: 1) that I should have had a real marketing strategy before I started my business and that I should not have created one as I go, 2) that I really should have been more knowledgeable about social media tools and how to use them, and lastly 3) that I needed an assistant to help me with my multiple detailed tasks that I didn't have time to do. I am a one woman show, so I do it all!

How do you keep yourself motivated and encouraged when things don't go right?

I keep myself motivated when things don't go right first by praying and asking for focus and direction. Then, by thinking about the impact that I'm making on people and how I'm setting an example for my teenage daughter who has some learning disabilities and she inspires me every day! She is very shy and quite but she works hard every day in school, and I try to be a role model to her and other members of my family. It is great to see when they are either looking for jobs or looking for career growth, that when they ask for advice from me and use it, it makes me proud! I want to help others shine! What also keeps me motivated is the thought of my Mom who I lost in 2008 and she was one of my biggest supporters and she would be proud of what I'm doing today. She would have been giving out my business cards everywhere she went. My Dad is a great supporter, and I'm blessed to have him at 84 years young. He is amazing and is healthy and living a full life.

What advice would you give to a woman in or near her fifties and older who wants to step out on her own and follow her dreams?

For women who are in or near their fifties, I say go for whatever it is you aspire to do"! It's never too late to pursue something you are passionate about. Age is just a number, and if you want it bad enough, you can achieve it. We can't let anyone discourage us from starting something at our age. I've had many people tell me that they admire my courage and motivation in starting something like what I do at my age. Some women in their fifties talk about finishing out their time in the jobs they have and retiring. This is okay if that is what you want, but we have choices in life. Yes, it is scary to start your own business or start a new career when you are in your fifties or above, but it is invigorating to step out on faith and take the plunge! I have no regrets and would not turn back now… I can honestly say that this is one of the best decisions I've made in my life. Surround yourself with your supporters and avoid those negative forces like the plague! My circles have changed tremendously, and if you want to be successful in business, you MUST surround yourself with like-minded people. We must have a "board of directors" not like in corporate America but this board are those you support you, give you feedback both good and bad, and have your best interest at heart.

I would recommend that all working professionals and business owners have a presence on LinkedIn. I have met so many wonderful contacts via that network. I think Facebook is another useful tool as well. I would recommend whatever works for you as far as meeting people, joining groups and organizations that support and relate to your areas of expertise. I am a networker, and it is crucial that I keep my networks open and wide. I share many of my contacts with my clients as well when needed. I have found much success in attending various networking events. This is a great way to meet people face to face and talk about what you do. I find that I have built some strong networks this way. I also think that webinars are great for obtaining further knowledge about specific topics especially when you can attend these in the privacy of your own home! One of the things I would suggest is to get certified in your craft; this is something I am working on but don't let that stop you from moving forward. Knowledge is power!

One of the biggest struggles that woman face when starting to pursue their dreams is dealing with the voices that tell them

"no", "It's too late," "no one will support you." Etc. What is the one thing that has helped you to overcome the battle of the voices and continue your journey?

I don't allow the voices that come and go in my head get away with breaking my spirit. I divert them to positive images of me and my family spending quality time together on vacation, or I meditate and listen to soft music. I tell myself there is no room for negativity and that I have to keep my eyes on the prize. I stay as far away as I can if I get negative vibes anywhere and everywhere I go. I have had many positive role models in my life, and it's also important to be one too.

You must have people within your circle that are knowledgeable about business or whatever your focus is, give you feedback both good and bad if needed which will help and not hinder you, and encourage and support you in your goals and objectives. I would recommend professionals that have expertise that you lack that will take your business/career/life to the next level.

What does Fierce Fabulous at Fifty Plus mean to you?

Fierce Fabulous at Fifty Plus means a great deal to me! I know that my life has started over, and I'm in charge of it! I never felt like this before, so I feel blessed to have had the opportunity to be at the head and not the tail of my career and yes, things aren't always easy but if you believe in yourself, no one can stop you! I am loving life and taking bold steps in doing what I love, and I wouldn't trade it for anything. I had some great jobs in my life, but the privilege of being a business owner is far greater. It also means that age is just a number, don't let it dictate who you are and what you do in life. This is a big world, and there is room enough for us all to succeed and to do this we must have confidence and a plan of action! I can't be afraid to allow my purpose in life to move me forward. I am grateful that I have lived a life filled with love, family, and success.

LET'S CONTINUE THE CONVERSATION
Leona Martin

Leona is a human resources professional with a wealth of knowledge and expertise in various aspects of this specialty. She was born and raised in the Boston area. She received a Master's degree in Education in 1992 from Cambridge College, which is located in Cambridge, Massachusetts. She currently has a career coaching business and works with individuals who are serious about reaching their career goals. Leona enjoys matching the right people to the right jobs.

She has a passion for partnering with both new and experienced professionals to develop plans of action to reach those career goals by marketing their skills, building self - confidence and by offering lots of encourage.

She is a woman of faith and believes that everyone has a purpose in life! Leona loves people and wants to make a difference in the lives of those who aspire to do great things.

Connect with Leona:

- Website - www.lcmcareercoaching.com
- Facebook - www.facebook.com/leonam2
- Twitter - @lcmcareercoaching
- LinkedIn - Leaona Martin

Fierce and Fabulous at Fifty Plus
Powerful Tip

Say "No" to things that you don't agree with, things that don't make you feel good and things that demand too much of you.

Set boundaries and don't allow people to take more from you than you have the mental capacity to give. Delegate responsibilities. Remember that if you feel the need to be in control of everything then everything has control of you. Your power is depleted when you are stressed and overworked.

Fierce and Fabulous at Fifty Plus
Peaceful Tip

Forgive others and remember that it doesn't mean that you should trust them. Forgive yourself. Stop holding yourself hostage to your mistakes and mess-ups.

Be slow to speak and don't react to everything you see. Have faith and let that be your guide. Learn to be driven internally and not externally.

AUDREY BLAKE
Founder, Fostering Leadership in You (FLY)

Tell us a little about yourself. We want to learn about the person behind the brand:

Born in Richmond, Virginia and raised in South Carolina, I grew up in the south and was shaped by southern values. I was the only child of an elementary school teacher and a general store owner. Hard work and integrity were instilled into me at an early age along with high achievement. After graduating from high school and college as a single parent, I landed a job at the local social service office as a case worker. There I became a licensed social worker.

I always wanted to help people be their best. I also wanted to make changes to the system that helped people so that it would be more efficient and effective. After several years of working in human services that included the University of South Carolina's School of Medicine and the Department of Health and Environmental Control, I went back to graduate school to study health administration. I pursued a degree that would help me land positions with decision –making power so that I could improve the system that serviced those in need. (A Master of Public Health)

Graduate school was a challenge. Since receiving my first degree (Bachelor of Arts in Psychology), I had gotten married and now had two sons. The marriage unfortunately only lasted seven years. I found myself attending graduate school, working full time as a manager at the local health department while doing a balancing act with my two sons ages 14 and 7. On so many days, I needed to clone myself as I had to be several places at the same time. Determined to get my Master of Public Health in Health Administration, I pushed forward. Frequently, I became physically ill as I was pushing my mind and body beyond the limits. The determination paid off. On May 8, 1998, I walked across the stage at the University of South Carolina and received my degree.

The next fifteen years were spent in a career of creating and directing health programs for women, infants, and children. I held positions that allowed me to create the policies and hire staff who were committed to helping others. In the process of promoting the programs, there were a lot of television and radio interviews. Programs to help teens make good choices were also created in schools and communities. I delivered many presentations along the way.

Feeling that my opportunities were maxed out in South Carolina, I moved to Ohio and accepted an Administrative position at the State Department of Health. This would be a position that I kept longer than any other job - almost nine years. While in Ohio, I continued to set standards to measure programs and ensure compliance with federal and state laws. It was during this time, that I also started writing my first book. I had experienced a lot of disappointments in relationships. Also, I noticed that my friends and some acquaintances were encountering unhealthy relationships. I thought back to the role plays that students did during my programs and noticed a trend. Many females were all dealing with the same issues in spite of their age, educational level or socioeconomic status.

In between work and family responsibility, I wrote chapters to the book that would highlight various experiences that women and young ladies may encounter in relationships. Over the course of 5 years in the evenings after work, and on weekends I wrote my thoughts down. Over time, this book became known as "Falling in Love with ME- Mutual Enhancement the Key to Healthy Fulfilling Relationships".

My life saw many changes while I lived in Ohio. I experienced the death of several family members. Many of them were men that had a purpose in my life such as my father and my favorite uncle. The greatest blow to me occurred in 2006 – the death of my true love, the father of my children who was then my ex-husband. He died at age 44. It was devastating. It was then, I realized that life was short, and we must go after dreams now and not put them off. In 2007, I officially registered my business (FLY-Fostering Leadership in You) with the Ohio Secretary of State's Office. I also submitted my completed manuscript, "Falling In Love With M.E. Mutual-Enhancement The Key To a Healthy Fulfilling Relationship" and sent it to a self-publishing company. The paperback was released in August 2007.

Sometimes what we think is a downfall may be the springboard to success. I took a position in Atlanta, Georgia and continued to run FLY part-time. I conducted seminars and conference workshops in between working in Atlanta. Then one day it happened. My position on my government job was eliminated. This could have been a devastating experience if I had perceived it as such. There was a feeling of relief as I read the letter informing me that my position was no longer needed. This was it! The opportunity to devote my full time and energy to building and expanding the company. I obtained my training and certification as a professional life coach, Now, I found myself in an ideal position to help my company FLY and Soar.

Each day I face new challenges in running and expanding the business. I am fueled by my motivation to make this a great company and leave a legacy for my children and future grandchildren. More importantly, every week I come across someone who shares with me how their lives have been impacted positively. It may be the motivation they received to complete a project, the push to start building their dreams, the encouragement to keep moving forward or the eye-opening experience gained from reading one of my books or hearing a keynote address. All of this gives me a true sense of satisfaction and purpose. It drives me to keep taking FLY higher and higher reaching the next level that God has planned. I don't always know the answers, but God provides the solutions. There have been times when this entrepreneurial journey has been scary, but I've learned to leap forward, and my wings are growing stronger as I soar. Life is too short to live with regrets and "what ifs". That is why I must continue to move ahead with the vision that God has given me.

Today, I encourage you, to move ahead with the vision God has been showing to you. Don't let the fear of failure or lack of resources hold you back. He has already lined up everything you will need along the way. Even your personal detours will ultimately prepare you for success. I speak from personal experience. God has allowed me to be used to accomplish many things in life- raising two successful young African –American sons, setting up programs to help those in the community among other things. For this, I am humbly grateful to be used. This new chapter of life, as FLY expands, is most exciting. There is nothing more fulfilling than walking in your passion, your calling. For that, I am forever grateful.

I Believed I Could FLY

Share with us what your business is and why you wanted to start this business.

FLY-Fostering Leadership In You is a consulting training and coaching company based out of Columbus Ohio and Atlanta, Georgia. The company offers Keynote Speaker Services, Empowerment Seminars, Professional Coaching Sessions and Coaching through radio talk show programming. Services are offered across the United States.

When did you know you were meant to launch your own business?

At least two years before the official launch, I knew that I had to create a forum outside of state government to help others excel and reach their goals. The company would give me the autonomy to make a difference and work around the barriers created by politics that I experienced in government. The death of my ex-husband propelled me to stop procrastinating because life indeed is short.

What has being in business for yourself done for you?

Being an entrepreneur has helped me to step out of my comfort zone and take risks for things that I believe in. When you are not dependent totally on your employer for outside revenue, there is a freedom that you will experience. Even if you work your business part-time at first, you will not find yourself rattled by your employer's talk of lay-offs and downsizing because you have another outlet for revenue with the potential for growth.

If someone asked you, who are your ideal clients, what would you say?

My clients are professionals, employers, college students, women and others who are aspiring to make a difference. These are clients that want to further their careers, enhance their skills, and improve their soft skills. I have clients that come to me because they want to write a book. Some use FLY services to conduct their employee workshops or conference seminars. Faith communities ask me to deliver keynote messages to singles groups or women's groups. My ideal client wants to be inspired.

How do you measure success and what is your definition of success?

Success is measured by two things: Accomplishment of Goals and self-fulfillment. Both of these are important. It is not enough to accomplish a goal. Many people accomplish goals and are not fulfilled. When a person feels personal fulfillment in their accomplishment, they are successful.

What was the biggest obstacle you've encountered since being in business? How did you overcome it?

The biggest obstacle in running the business has been finances. I have had to use a lot of my personal finances while expanding. I realize that any good business requires investments and over time with the right strategies it pays off. You must believe in your success more than anyone else. You must also be open to the advice of others who have gone before you. No one can be great alone. Draw from the wisdom of others.

What have you learned about yourself in running your business?

Running my business has revealed both my strong points and the opportunities for improvement. It allowed me to take a true look in the mirror and face life head on. I now hold myself to the same standards that I hold others.

What was your most rewarding experience since starting your own business?

Seeing my clients reach their goals and celebrating the milestones as they move closer toward their goals is very rewarding. When I sit down with a client, and we develop a measurable plan with timelines and seeing them carry out the activities and strategies while dealing with life events and sometimes interruptions, gives me such joy. I enjoy celebrating their successes.

What three things do you now wish you would've known when you started?

There are three things that I would share with someone thinking about starting their own business:
1. It takes hard work and perseverance.
2. Expect the unexpected and unplanned detours
3. Never give up on your dreams.

How do you keep yourself motivated and encouraged when things don't go right?

As a Certified Life Coach, I always tell clients that you have to believe in yourself more than anyone else. You must be your biggest cheerleader. I remind myself of why I started this company and the mission of the company.

What's your biggest business goal over the next 12 months and what will you do to meet it?

The company will expand its current services and aim to reach more clients. Marketing will play a major role in this process.

What advice would you give to a woman in or near her fifties that wants to step out on her own and follow her dreams of becoming and entrepreneur?

The first thing I would ask her is to examine her motivation. Once she is certain that her desire is coming from a place of integrity and not a substitution for an unaddressed area of her life. Then I would encourage her to get with a certified life coach and set goals and develop a plan. Most importantly I would encourage her to not let anyone kill her dreams.

One of the biggest struggles women entrepreneurs have is how to price themselves. What advice would you share about pricing your services and offerings?

Do your research on the market price for your product or services. Do not underestimate your work or your worth. Also take quality assurance seriously so that the service or product that your company delivers meets the standards and pricing levels. Seek to exceed expectations.

One of the biggest struggles that woman face when starting to pursue their dreams is dealing with the voices that tell them "no", "It's too late," "no one will support you." Etc. What is the one thing that has helped you to overcome the battle of the voices and continue your journey?

I have always had an inner confidence that I could do anything that I put my mind to do. This was instilled in me by my mother, Phyllis Blake, who died earlier this year (2015). I would tell women to not listen to the dream-killers. Believe in your vision and believe that if God gave it to you, he will give you all that you need to accomplish your mission in life. He never said it would be easy, just possible. Once you are sure of your dream and calling, go for it with everything in you.

What must have resources would you recommend to use in your business?

Start with your state's Small Business Administration. Many have a one-stop shop online with many valuable resources. You will also need a great accountant (CPA) and attorney. Also, there are many templates online and programs that will help you establish your business.

What does Fifty-ish, Fabulous, and Fierce mean to you?

I discovered that life begins at fifty. I am proud to be Fifty-ish, Fabulous, and Fierce! Reaching 50 unleashed a new freedom and confidence that was waiting to come out. By this age, I have experienced many things in life and learned many lessons along the way. My children are grown and independent. I find myself in an invaluable position to branch out and follow my dreams to wherever they lead. Fifty is fabulous. I'm looking better and feeling better inside and out. Being fifty-ish is fierce because I am unstoppable. Determination is stronger than ever. There may be times when setbacks attempt to discourage you, but you draw from past experiences and tell barriers...."I've met you before, and you don't scare me. So move out of my way!" You have an all-around confidence and care less and less about what people think of your goals and dreams. It is more important what God has planned for you than what people think you should be doing.

I am a certified professional life coach who coaches clients throughout the country who are writing their first book. I'm also a radio show host/co-host on a relationship and sexuality talk show who conducts seminars and speaking engagements across the United States. At the time of the writing this book, I have authored two paperback books, four e-books and completed a 400 page novel under publication. (Dying To Wake Up). I am the proud mother of two successful New opportunities are springing up daily. I accredit all of my success to God. Trusting God to lead your path and being open to going to in directions you never dreamed of and will leave you amazed at what can happen in your life. I often say to others "God's plans are bigger than your dreams. Run after your dreams. When you reach the cliff, don't give up. Take the leap. Do it afraid if you have to, and believe that you can fly.

Find out more or contact Audrey Blake at www.fosteringleaders.org for speaking engagements.

The End.

Adult sons, Maurice Jr. and Blake. Their father, Maurice Sr. is now deceased and I am dating. I believe in a healthy well-rounded balanced life.

LET'S CONTINUE THE CONVERSATION
Audrey Blake

Audrey is the founder and CEO of FLY (Fostering Leadership In You). The company was created in 2007 based on her passion for helping others succeed and has served hundreds through seminars and speaking engagements. She is a sought after guest speaker and has appeared on numerous radio and television shows. She currently co-hosts the weekly blog talk radio show "All About Relationships" The Dr. Jesse Walker Show.

She is the author of two books -"Falling In Love With M.E. Mutual Enhancement" and her newly released eBook "Dying To Wake Up" written under the pen name Marci. Her motto is to make a difference and make it happen.

Connect with Audrey:

- Website: www.fosteringlesaders.org
- Facebook: www.facebook.com/audreyb.lifecoach

Fierce and Fabulous at Fifty Plus
Confident Tip

Don't allow other people to pull you down when they say negative things about you. It's an ill reflection of them, and it isn't about you. Speak well to yourself, about yourself and about your world.

If you stumble and fall, get up, brush yourself off and get back on your journey. Now if you can walk on water, then you have no business falling! Hey, we all fall...welcome to the human race. Don't be so hard on yourself.

Fierce and Fabulous at Fifty Plus
Authentic Tip

Don't copy anyone else. "There's nothing like the real thing baby!" If God wanted us to duplicate other folk, then He would've done it Himself and created two in the first place. He knew what He was doing when He created each one of us; He doesn't need your help.

Don't allow yourself to be discouraged by what you see in someone else. Remember that you are on the outside looking in. You don't know the real story. Many people only show you what they want you to see....the good. They don't show you their struggles and pain. You don't see their pitfalls and heartaches. Know that you are more than enough, you are significant, and God needs you to be you, not anyone else.

SHERRI GLISSON
Founder, Fierce and Fabulous at Fifty Plus

With over 15 years as a Corporate Facilitator, Training Professional, Motivational Speaker and Coach, Sherri is passionate about helping Individuals, Professionals, Executives and Managers achieve their desired results.

Sherri is an energetic speaker that engages her audiences with her radiant personality, humor, and creative style. She inspires and moves her participants by sharing her life experiences and providing practical application and guidance.

She provides specialty coaching for Individuals who want to THRIVE and not just survive. She's committed to helping them on their journey to a better understanding of self by providing keys to help them unlock their gifts, realize their potential and live their lives from the inside out. **"Learning to listen to my internal voice versus being moved by what was happening externally has been liberating beyond what I could ever express in words"!** ~~Sherri G.

With over 15 years of working in Corporate America, transitioning from one position to the next and then stepping into the world of entrepreneurship, Sherri understands firsthand the uncertainty, fear and reluctance that Professionals may feel when they desire to make the shift, but aren't sure about what/where next. She is committed to helping them understand their gifts, realize their purpose and set realistic goals that will move them from where they are to where they are meant to be.

"I tried doing this on my own, but I became frustrated and almost gave up." "Investing in a Coach was one of the BEST things that I have ever done for myself,"~~Sherri G.

Sherri's specialties include workshops, coaching and team building programs for Executives and Mangers that are looking to realize an uptick in employee morale, motivation, and retention and an increase in sales and profits. "Amazing leaders know that the employees make the brand,"~~ Sherri G.

Fierce and Fabulous at Fifty Plus
Proactive Tip

Take action for your life. Don't allow yourself to be idle when people don't keep their promise or follow through. Your life and your dream are your responsibility.

Find out what you can do now to make things happen in your life. You may not have the funds to do what you can right now but what can you do.....research, attach yourself to a community of people that are where you want to be. Ask for help.

Fierce and Fabulous at Fifty Plus
Unstoppable Tip

Don't allow yourself to become overworked and stressed. Take the time to rest and relax. Get out and have some fun.

Create a vision board and use that to keep you close to your dream.....speak life to your dream, feel the excitement as if you were there right now!

This project has been an amazing blessing for me in many ways. I have stretched in ways I didn't even imagine and most importantly, I have shared with so many incredible woman that are fifty and plus in the last several months since beginning this journey.

The need for my connection to other woman who are transitioning or have transitioned to this brand new fierce and fab side of life was the catalyst for everything that has taken place in recent months. This book is the first in a brand new series of the Fierce and Fabulous At Fifty Plus. If you are a woman and you fit in this community and feel the need to share your story. Please reach out and let's go about the business of blessing other woman with your life.

As a speaker and coach, I offer programs that speak to the needs of many. However I am especially fond of working with women who are fifty and over.

Here is a sneak peek of what my programs offer:

At age 50 I was in the biggest battle of my life. I was lost. I was wandering around fighting for my purpose, and then it happened -- I shimmied into my armor like my last pair of jeans and took each rock thrown my way and turned it into my brick house. Through my journey of negative self-talk, missiles being shot at me left and right, friends tearing me down to make their building bigger – I learned a huge lesson. I wouldn't be the woman I am today without all those experiences.

I battled with low self-esteem that was triggered years ago during my childhood. I was a quiet child and people often mistook that as y being shy. I never felt like my voice really mattered, and I never wanted to take the spotlight in anything because I didn't feel good enough. This caused pain in my relationships. That was my first marriage that ended in a very short couple of years. A few months prior to turning age 50 I had an awakening and realized that I was the cause of my anguish and pain. How's that you ask? I was looking on the outside for what should have been already on the inside. At the time of this awakening, I was going through major trials in my life. My yearning for more saved my life! It wasn't literal. I was delivered from a drab existence. I overcame the "dead woman walking" syndrome!

During this time, I sought out a community jam-packed with fun, vibrant women in their 50+, and I was saddened because I did not find one that was quite the Cinderella fit. I wanted a place where women felt the vibrations of what life is like after fifty, a place where we are not only celebrated, uplifted and supported but a place where we could receive valuable information that was simple and easy to execute.

Here I am 5 years later -- I created a place where women were supported and helped one another step into their greatest expression of themselves….A place where each one has a voice is significant and where no woman is left alone. Transitioning at midlife can be difficult and especially when you feel like all hope is lost.

In this community, we talk about the REAL life stuff that everyone shy's away from. We are going talk about the "OMGoodness, where have the kids gone?" to "Why on earth am I so hot all of a much more. Yes, to the bottom of fabulousness is sudden?" to so so we will get down w h y   o u r contagious!

I'm a very vibrant and I know you **fiftyish woman, are too!**

Join me and other and 50+ women as world! fabulous, fierce, we take on the

Fierce and Fabulous at Fifty Plus
Fabulous (Means extraordinary) Tip

Remember that you are an original. It's okay to be different because you were created that way. The reason the ordinary, mundane and routine is driving you batty is because you were created to be and do more.

Learn what your gifts are. Your gifts are not the same as your skills. Many people don't know the difference, so they get jobs and work in which they are skilled at and before you know it the thrill is gone. When you operate using your gifts and step into your unique purpose, your life is much more enriching.

Sapphire Membership: (Yearly Subscription)
Membership Benefits:

Tuesday Mornings with Sherri –
* Every Tuesday morning, you will receive a dose of "Tuesday Mornings with Sherri" be warned, I keep it real. All days are not pretty days, but all days are fillable with love, kindness, and the spirit to keep going. I can't wait to share Tuesday morning tea or coffee with you!

Connect with women "Just like you" –
* You will be strutting in a community of women that "get it". You've been around the block and have seen and experienced things that these youngin's have not. You will be in a community where others are cheering you on and provide a sacred, safe zone where you can laugh, cry, vent

and let it all out. The community is here to walk with you not against you.

Realistic tools to help deal with life changing challenges –
* Look, I know there are a million gazillion things out there. Within this community, we tell you what worked for us. You will receive tools and resources that will help you live with empty nesting or those hot flashes that got you all worked up.

Discover Your Inner Power –
* You will learn what your gifts and how to tap into them to create your ideal life. You will be able to cut out the negativity, tell people no with ease, strut in your heels like the woman you have always been (she s just been hiding.) Learn to live a healthy, less stressful life filled with joy and happiness.

Empowerment and Purpose –
* Zeroing in on your unique gifts and skills that will give you the freedom to live your life by your standards.

* Become unstuck, clear and focused –

* Remove the brick walls before you, set boundaries and stop kicking yourself in the behind for the coulda, woulda, shoulda's.

Diamond Membership (Yearly Subscription)

You will receive EVERYTHING in the SAPPHIRE level PLUS:

- **Semi-Annual Group Coaching Session with SherriG (value $997) –**
  - The swiftness of group sessions will have your heart pulsating for more every time. Our sessions together will tackle challenges and concerns that are hindering group members. Each member is dedicated to supporting, sharing perspective, offering advice (when desired) share resources and strategies. The power of an accountability alliance will help each of use stay off the crazy train and stay motivated and on target to reach our individual goals. The fierce and fabulousness energy is so contagious; doctors will need to start handing out prescriptions.

- **VIP invitation to participate in the *Fifty-ish, Fabulous And Fierce (And Then Some)* as a co-author at a lower cost.**
  - You will be sitting alongside your 50+ sisters who have a story to tell. Stories are meant to be told, and there is no story quite like yours. When you co-author with this book, you will join forces with women who are standing in their purpose and have one ultimate mission: To reach as many women possible who are 50+ live the best days of their lives NOW!

So that's just a run-down of what my community programs are about. To find out more, you can contact me at info@sherrigspeaks.com and www.sherrgspeaks.com.

Reach out to find out more and thanks BUNCHES for supporting us!

www.ingramcontent.com/pod-product-compliance
Lightning Source LLC
LaVergne TN
LVHW021538080426
835509LV00019B/2714